Homing In

Homing In

Poems by Mo Gallaccio
Images by Maureen Morris

Paekakariki Press
Walthamstow
2011

this is number 85......
of a limited edition of
1 5 0 copies

© *2011, Mo Gallaccio*

set in
12pt Garamond
by Speedspools, Edinburgh
and printed at

Paekakariki Press
Walthamstow
2011

ISBN: 978-1-908133-01-4

Homing In

What I love about death is

she's inclusive
up for everyone
without exception

> no more
> shivering on the side lines
> waiting
> sick
> scared
> I'll not get picked
> again

the Buddhist monk on the Byers road
looks cold in saffron cheesecloth
but the Oxfam will provide
woolly socks and jumpers
even hats with earflaps

I'm relaxed
knowing one day
my turn will come
and she'll be there
face neon white
arms outstretched in welcome
to envelope me completely
in that big black knitted poncho
clasp me and squeeze
the living daylights
out of me

> so until then
> I'll just get on
> looking for nirvana

Behind the Door

two coats, one winter weight, one necessary mac —
time snaps back like elastic
I'm in that street of neatly tailored serviceable
two-up two-downs snug as a bug.

Front doors open straight on the street
women with wraparound arms talking,
me out the back, playing in clean dirt
four-year-old fingers grubbing for caterpillars.

My Gran's peg is empty — in her flecked tweed
and headscarf turban, she's nipping round the
    neighbours,
pinch of gossip, twist of tea — the fire banked with
    slack
the black iron kettle, full and ready on the hob.

Night-time stories, prone on the rag rug as Gran runs
    through
its hooked-in histories, who wore what when,
dreamy I watch the shifting pictures in the coals
while sparks fly up as the wind huffs down.

3

Homing In

She'll be in the kitchen, he'll be somewhere else.
Red-rare roast beef the way he likes it.
I hear the silence.

Like a black and white movie the room fills
with a big band sound — they are fox-trotting
ready to take a gamble.

A splinter of ice is dislodged in my chest,
me in a pink smocked frock, she sparkly in midnight
   blue.
We are all wearing smiling faces.

Quick
tie a knot in the hankie,
retrace my steps.

5

Pianoforte

(After Edward Hopper)

The piano
its back to the wall
endures silence.

Eager for tunes,
black and white keys
huddle in groups.

He studies markets
profits or loss
I'm invisible in poppy-red silk.

The upright piano and I
hate silence
with the forefinger of my right hand

choosing D above middle C
quiet, but insistent
I tap out SOS

Montrose

white sand, wind, goose bumps,
a woman knits, the Aran tree of life:
I'm cold! Bury me! Children
come running to cover her,
half woman/half fish, dressing
the tail with shells, fronds of weed

absorbed in mazes, castles
combing the shore, they jump
shallow pools — a sideways scutter
of crabs; join hands with the woman
run to the edge of the sea
footsteps weaving, dancing

a bus ride home;
into the bath, silt of sand,
boiled from mottled blue to lobster,
costumes flapping on the line
Pink sky tonight,
Shepherds Delight!

Wired to the cold moon,
the sea foams
round the indent of their dancing,
rakes through the pebbles,
sighs and seuchs,
swallows all traces

Montrose (ii)

On hard benches,
damp, we wait
till the tent fills with a chatter of folk.
The plain woman
who sold us tickets on the door, transforms
into the tightrope walker.
Spangled
supple as a seal
she slides into the splits,
juggled hoops whir
and blur to white.

Mighty Oleg from the Steppes
broader than he's tall
grunts and sweats, bends girders with his neck.
A troupe of Chinese acrobats
airy as birds
run up each other
flip over
grow
into a human tower.
The catcher holds the first man by the knees —
teetering,
he keeps them all
balanced.

The ringmaster
a woman majestic on a horse shiny as conkers
waltzes with Shetland ponies,
packs of excited poodles hurtle though hoops
the clowns do that old falling into the crowd
with a bucket of water routine, we four shriek
and huddle
are showered with confetti.

They've taken their bows
we file out, tired
itchy with sand, tetchy,
head for home
spy Mr and Mrs O,
ordinary again:
she pegs out a wash behind the van
he peels spuds in an enamel bowl.

Deserted
the canvas tent strains like a beast,
coarse grass whips and cracks.
White horses buck and break
snaking up the shore,
tumbling sea-polished pebbles
over the shingle
like dice.

Single file

a man and a woman walk along a road
the man is in front
    he hums and whistles

the woman some paces behind
wrestles with thoughts and feelings
tries to pin them to words

exploratory phrases go unheard
    a) because he is deaf
    b) because he is not wearing his aid
    c) because he is communing with his inner self

the woman persists
a drawer full of old unacknowledged words
flies open
letters spill out

words hang in the space
some fall and are ground to dust
some take flight and catch on the branches of trees
some soar nearer the sun

the man and the woman walk on

II

The Purple Iris

For Mark and in memory of Shun-Wah Chan

Morning
    the purple iris amazes me again,
not washed out lilac, not
in-your-face indigo
just absolute, imperial rex
perfect purple.
A yellow runway for the bees,
corduroy ribbed, to rob them of their pollen
but just in case, beckoning moth markings
faint fawn of thrush feathers, pointing,
nudging the way to the dark sweet centre.

Noon
    my downstairs neighbours
are back from the hospital: in shock.
A rare tumour is growing behind her face.
I see mauve plums ripening.
He details surgical procedures.
My mouth dries with clichés.

Night
        no sleep, the impervious moon
still rises, one fat moth batters and batters
against cold glass. Old scars unhealed
tear open.

If we could get back, to that last
moment, the moment before
the knowledge that fractures —
        I want to dive into the iris
        lose myself in colour
let the purple bear me up.

        *   *   *

For two hard years I watched my young friend
fight. She lost. No miracle occurred.
My son stays dead.

The seasons tick round.
Lavender heals
with purple sage and the modest
creeping viola, heartsease
life-bruises fade
and almost disappear.

The purple iris still amazes —
without fail
it takes my breath away.

Snapshot

Where are you?
I can't place it.
I remember the frock
fawn and brown check
M&S, smart, easy to care for,

your hair brown and fawn
a discreet rinse: nice set
swept back from that wide broad brow. I'll bet
you slept the previous night in curlers.
    You have to suffer to be beautiful.

A beer glass in your hand
resting against your lips
masking an enigmatic Mona Lisa
smirk, and behind those fly away
specs, your eyes are hooded
mocking, focused somewhere else
your whole demeanour saying
    There's a world of things about me
    that you'll never know!

Too right — the questions never asked
for fear I wouldn't like the answers?
The information never volunteered:
your northern reticence and stubborn pride.

Now way too late, I try to comprehend
your life. Your hopes, the choices that you made
the ones made for you —
    Come lady luck and smile on me today!
She rarely did.

I hold a photo of a middle-aged woman
and I begin to see you.

Present

You've gone, caught your train.
I'm back.
        The house is much the same,
but the air is frantic, arranging and re-
arranging molecules and atoms
to take account of
        absence.

The room is out of sorts. Chairs
turn from the table, rugs pull up
from the floor, and the magnificent overblown
tulips, are finally
naked stalks
amongst drooping leaves.

I hope
for comfort.
        In the fridge
a last wedge of watermelon
        just one bite taken,
your smile
embedded in
        pink sherbet flesh.

Sunlight allelujahs
        round the kitchen.
The rooms are for living in again.

Sweet present.

16

Summer

In their pens the watermelons are restive,
vying for attention, voluptuous,
showing off their curves. Dark
perfect globes, resonant as tom toms
luxuriating in the heat, shameless,
radiating sun and *come and get me*.
A tiger striped giant winks furiously:
smitten, I scoop it up,
hug it to me and lug
it home, precariously
balanced on one hip.

The kitchen cools with shadows.
My prize, trembling on a platter,
sponged clear of dust,
sweats gratitude and torpor.
Calmly reassuring, lending my weight,
I steady it with my left hand,
and with my right
and an old bread knife make
swift, surgical incisions.

A gasp, a sigh,
oh thankful to be freed
it relaxes into

vivid

joyous

fleshy

grins.

The Dancin'

Are you out the night?
Aye. Chum me?
Aye. After wur tea.
See ye.
Cold ham and beetroot covered by a plate
wait. Her note — I've left some tinned fruit.
Mind you lock up and don't be late back.
See ye.

Luxury. Oh unexpected Privacy,
I tango to the bathroom and take all
the hot water. In the steam dream tonight
will be the night I turn into a swan.
Aw go on.
Is that the time? Look at my hair!
Up in a pony tail — I don't care.
What'll I put on? My blue will do.
Hell's bells I think I've lost my shoe.
A squoosh of Mum's Yardley's behind each ear.
Saved by the bell — Maggie's here.
Hair held captive by a chiffon square,
eyes lined, cheeks rouged. *Are we right?*
Are we ready? Are we off? Aye.
Arm in arm we sashay shrieking up the street.
See us!

Ladies cloaks — what a crush.
Who are you saving the last dance for Doreen?
Mind yer own!
Anyone seen Wilma? What's she like!
Dressed like that for a bet or what?
See her!

Sat at the edge, back to the wall,
I panic — supposin' nobody comes for me.
Sandy Andy McKendrick
second year apprentice mechanic,
freckles fiery in a milk white face,
stands out in a crowd — lanky and loud
has come for Mags.
Are you dancin'? Are you askin'?
I'm askin — and she's away.
Stately as a small galleon
French pleat and double starched petticoats,
she turns with a wink
See ye.

I concentrate on minding her seat,
one eye on the door.
Suddenly — the boy Robertson,
James, back from the Uni
in a smart blue blazer,
is crossing the floor.
He gives a wee bow.
Would you care to? Holds out his arm,
I rise, clumsy and clammy, step on his feet.
Shall I count us in? I nod.
His arm, round my waist, not tight but firm,
mine on his shoulder.
Palm to palm, eye to eye,
deep breath in and
weight on the toes, bend the knee, slide
two and three glide
turn and — we're off we're away
he smiles, so do I.
Holy moly Mags
See me!
I'm dancin'.

Acknowledgements

Thanks to Barbara Hardy for choosing and editing the poems for this collection. *Summer* and *The Dancin'* were previously published in *Magma*. *The Purple Iris* was previously published in *Artemis Poetry*.